JESUS— FOR THE *REST* OF YOUR LIFE

by Dr. James McKeever

*This booklet is dedicated
first and foremost
to the glory of God
and of His Son, Jesus Christ.*

JESUS—FOR THE *REST* OF YOUR LIFE

Copyright © 1989 by James M. McKeever

Printed in the United States of America
First Printing August, 1989

Omega Publications
P. O. Box 4130
Medford, Oregon 97501 U.S.A.

Special rates for bulk orders and for bookstores.

ISBN 0-86694-116-9

JESUS—FOR THE *REST* OF YOUR LIFE

These are troubled times and they are likely to become even more troubled. There are many tensions that exist, both on international and domestic fronts. Yet in such a troubled world, a Christian should have no anxiety and no fear, but rather internal peace. This is one of the most precious gifts that the Lord Jesus left with us. Because of this, it appears to be the favorite thing that Satan, the thief, tries to steal from Christians most often. If you have an occasional lack of peace or sometimes feel troubled, frustrated or anxious over the world and economic situation, then perhaps you are the one that the Lord is having me write this booklet for. Let's take a look at peace. Perhaps the Holy Spirit can use these words to not only restore any peace that you may have lost, but to cause peace to permanently abide within your heart.

LOVE—JOY—PEACE

In Galatians 5, where it talks about the fruit of the Spirit, the first three listed are love, joy, and peace. In another booklet entitled *Only One Word*, we looked at the love that a young man has for a young lady and compared that to the love that we should have for God. If we truly love someone, we want to talk to that person, be with him, read about him, please him, and tell everyone how wonderful he or she is. In that booklet, we pointed out that loving God is the key to the Christian life. If we love Him with all of our heart, soul and mind, the totality of our Christian life will fall into place.

I would like to take that analogy two steps further by again looking at that young man and young lady. After they have fallen in love and know that they are loved equally as much in return, what is the result of that love? The answer is *real joy!* The young man runs along, jumping into the air, clicking his heels together, shouting, either out loud or to himself, "She loves me! She loves me! . . . She really *loves* me!" What a joy it is to love and be loved by another human being!

We need to ask ourselves the question, will we experience this same kind of joy, perhaps even more so, if we really fall in love with God and if we become aware of the immensity, the strength, and the depth of His love for us? I think the answer is yes—that we *will* experience this kind of joy. (Just as an aside, if you are a Christian who seems to have a lack of joy, I would suspect that it comes from this root source of not really loving God enough and not being as aware of *His* love as you should be.) If you ask Him to help you to love Him with all of your heart, soul and mind, and to make you aware of how much He loves and cherishes you, the joy will follow as naturally as day follows night.

Again returning to the story of the young man and young lady, after the exuberant burst of joy that first comes from knowing that they are in love and that the love is returned, the joy remains but it mellows and becomes deeper. In fact, the intensity of it should grow stronger, even though the exhibition of it might become quieter. What then follows after joy, as the relationship between this young man and young lady moves toward marriage and beyond? The answer is peace.

The restlessness of a continual search for a life partner is over and peace takes its place. The insecurities of the dating years are gone. There is no more wondering, "Does she love me? Will we be together forever?" In its place is peace. There is a surety that this wonderful relationship—through ups and downs, through thick and thin—will continue for the rest of their lives. There is peace—a deep and abiding peace that allows this young couple to sit together looking at a sunset, quietly holding hands, not even needing to speak. There is such beauty in this peace that has its genesis and its foundation in love. The young man might even be going off to war the next day, but while he is with his loved one he has this beautiful internal peace, and so does she.

PEACE FROM LOVING GOD

If we really love God and are aware of His love, do you think that peace inside our hearts will follow? I think it will. We certainly would have this peace as long as are "with Him". How are we "with the Lord"? I believe we are with Him as we talk to Him, as we are conscious of His presence, and—as Psalm 1 says—as we meditate in His law day and night. As long as our mind is conscious of Him and His presence, we will have peace. This was said so beautifully by Isaiah, the Prophet:

3   Thou wilt keep him in perfect peace, whose mind is stayed on thee: because he trusteth in thee.
—Isaiah 26 (KJV)

You may want to reread that verse several times and even memorize it. After you have done that, ask yourself the question, "Do I want perfect peace?" If you do, this verse tells you how to get it—by simply setting your mind steadfastly on the Lord and trusting in Him.

Trusting Him to do what? Trust Him to do the very best by you and to look out for your happiness. If you are really convinced that God loves you and wants the best for you, you can relax and rest (be at peace). You don't have to worry about figuring out your life or your finances; nor do you have to have anxiety over the world situation or be up tight over the situation at work. You can cuddle up in God's arms, knowing that He will take care of you, provide for you, and give you those things which will make for your maximum happiness. You can also be comforted by His protection and thus have no need to fear anything—not war, not persecution, not economic collapse . . . not anything—if you live conscious of Him and His love.

The fact that nothing can separate us from the love of God and the love of Christ is pointed out beautifully in Romans 8:

> 35   Who shall separate us from the love of Christ? Shall tribulation, or distress, or persecution, or famine, or nakedness, or peril, or sword?
> 36   Just as it is written,
>   "FOR THY SAKE WE ARE BEING PUT TO
>   DEATH ALL DAY LONG;
>   WE WERE CONSIDERED AS SHEEP TO BE
>   SLAUGHTERED."
> 37   But in all these things we overwhelmingly conquer through Him who loved us.
> 38   For I am convinced that neither death, nor life, nor angels, nor principalities, nor things present, nor things to come, nor powers,
> 39   nor height, nor depth, nor any other created thing, shall be able to separate us from the love of God, which is in Christ Jesus our Lord.

Isn't that beautiful? Absolutely nothing can separate us from the love of God. Not guns, nor tanks, nor nuclear bombs, nor demons, nor anything to be created in the future—not even death can separate us from the love of God! If we were aware of how much He loves us and what He was willing to do by allowing Jesus to die so that we could spend eternity with Him, we would never again be afraid of anything. This is pointed out in 1 John 4:

> 18   There is no fear in love; but perfect love casts out fear, because fear involves punishment, and the one who fears is not perfected in love.

This love isn't something that we have to generate. It is being *aware* of *God's* perfect love that will cast any fear out of your heart and in its place put a beautiful, perfect peace. Christ Himself pointed out that the peace that He was going to give to us was the opposite of being troubled, anxious and fearful:

> **27** "Peace I leave with you; My peace I give to you; not as the world gives, do I give to you. Let not your heart be troubled, nor let it be fearful. . . ."
>
> —John 14:27

Christ said that He was leaving His peace with us. It is a gift from Him to you and rightfully belongs to you. There should never be a moment when you are without peace. If you find yourself with a lack of peace then Satan, through whatever means, has stolen your peace from you. At that point in time you can bind Satan, in the name of Christ, and you can loose your peace and it will return to you. Praise God!

This is not a peace that only exists when one is looking at beautiful sunsets. This is a peace that endures through any kind of turmoil. Christ knew that He was going to be tortured to death when He said these words:

> **33** "These things I have spoken to you, that in Me you may have peace. In the world you have tribulation, but take courage; I have overcome the world."
>
> —John 16

He was saying that His peace that He was leaving with us was the kind of peace that remains in spite of tribulation, or in spite of the fact that one might be facing death by torture. This peace that He offers to us is one that abides *regardless* of circumstances. Isn't that wonderful? Thank you, Lord!

HOW DO I GET THIS PEACE?

Since this peace is a gift that Christ gave to His disciples, the first and foremost requirement to have it is that you know Christ as your Savior and are one of His followers. In addition, we have already mentioned one other thing: you must keep your mind steadfastly on God and His love.

There is another thing that is involved in having God's peace and this is found in Romans 8:

5   For those who are according to the flesh set their minds on the things of the flesh, but those who are according to the Spirit, the things of the Spirit.
6   For the mind set on the flesh is death, but the mind set on the Spirit is life and peace, . . .

13   for if you are living according to the flesh, you must die; but if by the Spirit you are putting to death the deeds of the body, you will live.
14   For all who are being led by the Spirit of God, these are sons of God.

In these verses we see that to have life and peace we need to be led by the Spirit of God. In fact, I believe that Romans 8:14 is the best definition of a Christian that I have found in the Bible. To me, being led by the Spirit means being controlled by the Holy Spirit (being baptized or filled with the Holy Spirit). This means that we are not doing our own thing, going our own way, making our own decisions (setting our minds on things that our body or flesh wants to do), but instead we are being controlled by God through the Holy Spirit. As we pointed out in the booklet *Only One Word*, if you love God with all of your heart, you are going to naturally want to please Him, which means obeying Him. These verses in Romans 8 reemphasize that this is a part of having the peace of God; you must be doing what He wants you to do.

For example, if God had told Joseph to store up seven years of grain and he did not do it, then he would not have had peace. If God had told Noah to build an ark and he had not obeyed, he would not have had peace. So even though perfect love casts out fear, and peace is a gift from God that no man can take away, we can take it away from ourselves by not following God. Thus, if we are walking moment by moment led by the Spirit and we make any preparations that He tells us to (build a bomb shelter, store food, store water, or do nothing), then we will have a peace, knowing that whatever comes we will be abiding in God's strong loving arms and will be protected by Him.

PEACE AND KNOWING THE WILL OF GOD

What we just talked about ties right into a subject that would now like to deal with, which is knowing the will of God. Probably the question I am asked more often as I travel around to speak is, "How do I know the will of God?" Let me share with you what I share with these dear brothers and sisters in Christ who ask me that.

There are really five ways that God can guide us and make his will known to us. Of the five ways, four are grouped together in one category and one is overwhelmingly the most important. I will list this most important one last, since we will deal with it last.

1. A multitude of counselors
2. Circumstances
3. The Bible
4. Direct guidance (visions, dreams or God's voice)
5. Peace in your heart

1. *A multitude of counselors*:   Let us look at these one at a time. In this first one we are simply restating what it says in Proverbs:

> 14   Where there is no guidance, the people fall,
> But in abudance of counselors there is victory.
> —Proverbs 11

The King James says that "in the multitude of counselors there is safety." God can guide us through the counsel of others (and I would include words of personal prophecy in this category), but it should never be the counsel of just one person or even two. I would say that if this is the way that God is going to guide you, there should be the counsel of a minimum of three godly righteous men, ideally independent of each other, and not necessarily part of the same body of believers. I want to underscore that they must be *godly, righteous* men. Psalm 1 admonishes righteous men not to "walk in the counsel of the ungodly". If you are taking advice in any area of your life from a non-Christian, you are walking in the counsel of the ungodly and violating what God tells you to do. I would include the financial area in this admonition. If you are taking financial advice from a non-Christian you are violating God's commands. Whether it be me or some other Christian financial counselor I would encourage you to switch and take the advice of Christians only. I think the same thing is true concerning your lawyer and CPA. These men should be Christians. If the matter is big enough, whether it be financial or legal, you should let them know that you are going to seek a "multitude of counselors". God can certainly use three or more Christian counselors to give you guidance.

2. *Circumstances*: God can use circumstances to guide us. If we are praying about going to college "A" or college "B" and college "A" rejects us and college "B" accepts us, God can use those closed doors to guide us. I emphasize closed doors and not open doors. I do not look at open doors as a way of God directing us, because each of us have thousands of doors open to us every day. *The need does not constitute the call.* If we were to look at needs around the world, and even in our own community or church, where we have the ability to meet the need, we could quickly become committed to 95 hours a day. So open doors I do not believe are a way that God uses to guide us. However, when God closes a door I think that we can rejoice in the fact that He has prevented us from doing something that wouldn't be best for us and give us the maximum happiness. Even though the door that He closes might be one that we very much wanted to walk through, we still need to praise Him for His loving care and guidance.

3. *The Bible*: When I say the Bible, I mean principles in the Bible and not a specific isolated verse. People have opened the Bible and read something about islands in a verse, and they took this as God calling them to be missionaries on an island. In such cases it usually turns out to be a disaster. But even in using principles of the Bible we have to be careful. One can use the Bible to make decisions that are independent of God. We can say to ourselves, "Well, the Bible says this;

therefore, I will do it", without ever asking God what He wants us to do.

4. *Direct guidance (visions, dreams or God's voice)*: God can guide us directly through a vision or a dream, a visit from an angel, or God speaking to us directly. This in some ways is the most dangerous of all of the ways of guidance because all of these things are also counterfeited by Satan. Therefore, we must have a confirmation from another source to know that it is from God. We know that God spoke to Joseph (Mary's husband) through a dream. He spoke to many people in both the Old and New Testaments through angels, and frequently God has spoken directly to an individual, such as Moses or Paul. This type of guidance directly from God is usually much more rare than the previously mentioned types.

5. *Peace in your heart*: The final umpire, the final decider, the final ruler as to whether a particular plan of action that God seems to be indicating is really His will or not is whether or not you have peace in your heart. This is pointed out in Colossians 3:

> **15   And let the peace of Christ rule in your hearts, to which indeed you were called in one body; and be thankful.**

No matter if a multitude of counselors are giving you direction in some area and the Bible seems to confirm it, if you do not have peace in your heart, do not do it. We can use this in many, many ways. In one of my books I mentioned the example of Barney Coombs, who is now a pastor in Vancouver, B.C. At the time of this incident he was a pastor in England. He was driving home one night. The road to his house forked and later the two roads joined back together. Thus, he could take either the left fork or the right fork, with the time and the distance being the same. He felt a strong urging to take the right fork. Most of us would have just done it without thinking. However, Barney prayed and said, "God, if I am to take the right fork and that is of You, give me a real peace inside, and if not, give me a real disquiet." In answer to that prayer, God gave him a real disquiet, so he took the left fork instead. A little way down that road he picked up a hitchhiker whom he had the privilege of leading to Christ. Satan, in the worst way, did not want him to take the left fork, and thus was giving him a strong urge to take the right fork.

We can use this technique in our daily lives. When we have a decision to make that may seem inconsequential such as who to have lunch with, we can ask God, "God, if you want me to have lunch with Joe then give me a real peace inside, and if not give me an unrest". God delights in this kind of prayer and delights in answering us.

Up until now we have just talked about guidance for an isolated individual. The same thing applies to more than one person. For example, if a husband and wife are both Christians, both seeking God's will, and are contemplating a particular action, I think God will give them *both* peace if it is His will for them to act in a certain manner. Similarly with a group of elders trying to arrive at a decision; if it is God's will, He will give them all perfect peace. What happens in a group of elders if four of them feel peace and the fifth one doesn't? In that situation one of two things are true:

1. It is not God's will that they take that particular action and He is using the fifth elder as a check to prevent them from making a mistake . . . or
2. The fifth elder has a spiritual problem that needs to be dealt with and is not hearing from God.

In either case I do not believe the action should be taken until there is perfect unity in the Spirit. It may be that the group needs to pause, deal with any spiritual problems among the elders and then reconsider the question. If everyone (or both people in a couple) do not feel perfect peace, either it is something they should not do or at least one party is not truly seeking to do God's will regardless of his own desires. Thus, God can use peace not only to direct individuals, but groups of people as well. Thank you, Lord, for this beautiful and simple way that You let us know if we are walking in Your will.

SUMMARY AND CONCLUSION

Let's see where we have come. The economic system of the world is in an upheaval. The likelihood of a military conflict is growing every day. There is trouble and violence around us on every side. There is even tension and difficulties between Christians. As the tribulation draws near, the prospect of persecution, famine and other things looms ahead of us. None of these things can separate us from the love of God.

As long as we are secure in loving God with all of our heart and are aware of His presence and of His tremendous love for us, then we can have perfect peace. This peace is a gift that Christ left for us and it rightly belongs to us. Satan will want to steal it from us, but as long as we have our eyes on God and are doing His will, we can claim and can have God's perfect peace.

God can use this peace as a final determining, confirming or overriding factor in our knowing His will for our lives, either in big things or in small day to day things. He can also use this peace to direct a group or to prevent a group from taking an action that is not the best for them.

Thus, no matter what comes, or how turbulent the world situation becomes (even if World War III started), Christians should and can dwell in perfect peace.

As we are filled with the fruit of righteousness, the fruit of the Holy Spirit, we should have so much love, joy and peace inside that it overflows to other people. So many visitors have commented when visiting here at Living Waters Ranch about what a sense of peace they have felt. I do not believe this is because of the physical piece of ground or the beautiful setting, but because the individuals here walk in the peace of God.

Our prayer for you is that when people come into your presence, you will be so filled with peace and love and joy that they will go away commenting that they had such a peaceful feeling when they were with you. Remember—you have an endless supply of peace because it is Jesus' peace that

He left with you. Grace and peace to you all. With much
love.

MEET THE AUTHOR

Dr. James McKeever is an international consulting economist, lecturer, author, world traveler and Bible teacher. His financial consultations are utilized by scores of individuals from all over the world who seek his advice on investment strategy and international affairs.

Dr. McKeever is the editor and major contributing writer of the *McKeever Strategy Letter*, an economic and investment letter with worldwide circulation and recognition, rated #1 for 1985, 1986 and 1988 by an independent newsletter-rating service, and showing an average profit of 66.25 percent per year over the eleven year period 1978-1988.

Dr. McKeever has been a featured speaker at monetary, gold and tax haven conferences in London, Zurich, Bermuda, Amsterdam, South Africa, Australia, Singapore and Hong Kong, as well as all over the North American continent and Latin America.

As an economist and futurist, Dr. McKeever has shared the platform with such men as Ronald Reagan, Gerald Ford, William Simon, William Buckley, Alan Greenspan, heads of foreign governments and many other outstanding thinkers.

For five years after completing his academic work, Dr. McKeever was with a consulting firm which specialized in financial investments in petroleum. Those who were following his counsel back in 1954 invested heavily in oil.

For more than ten years he was with IBM, where he held several key management positions. During those years, when IBM was just moving into transistorized computers, he helped that company become what it is today. With IBM, he consulted with top executives of many major corporations in America, helping them solve financial, control and information problems. He has received many awards from IBM, including the "Key Man Award" and the "Outstanding Contribution Award." He is widely known in the computer field for his books and articles on management, management control and information sciences.

In addition to this outstanding business background, Dr. McKeever is an ordained minister. He has been a Baptist evangelist, pastor of Catalina Bible Church for three and a half years (while still with IBM) and a frequent speaker at Christian conferences. He has the gift of teaching and an indepth knowledge of the Bible, and has authored fourteen best-selling Christian books, seven of which have won the "Angel Award."

Dr. McKeever is president of Omega Ministries, which is a non-profit organization established under the leading of the Holy Spirit to minister to the body of Christ by the traveling ministry of anointed men of God, through books, cassettes, seminars, conferences and video tapes. He is the editor of the widely-read newsletter, *End-Times News Digest* (published by Omega Ministries), which relates the significance of current events to biblical prophecy and to the body of Christ today. The worldwide outreach of Omega Ministries is supported by the gifts of those who are interested.

WRITING TO THE AUTHOR

If this booklet, JESUS—FOR THE *REST* OF YOUR LIFE, has made an impact on your life, you may want to write to Dr. McKeever in the space below.

Also, on the reverse side are shown some of his other materials and services.

Comments:

TO:

DR. JAMES McKEEVER
OMEGA MINISTRIES
P. O. BOX 4130
MEDFORD, OR 97501 USA

Dear Dr. McKeever,
I am enclosing:

☐ $________ for additional copies of JESUS—FOR THE *REST OF YOUR LIFE* (for a contribution of $1.95 each)

☐ $________ for your ministry in general

☐ $________ Total contribution enclosed
(make check payable to Omega Ministries)

☐ I will be praying for your ministry

NAME _______________________________________

ADDRESS ____________________________________

CITY ____

STATE _________________________ ZIP ___________

PHONE _______________________________________

Also send me information on the following materials by Dr. James McKeever:

☐ Other booklets in this series
☐ The Christian newsletter that he edits, *End-Times News Digest (END)*
☐ Books by him
☐ Cassettes of his speaking ministry
☐ Information about his speaking at our church or Christian conference
☐ Please read comments on other side

WRITING TO THE AUTHOR

If this booklet, JESUS—FOR THE *REST* OF YOUR LIFE, has made an impact on your life, you may want to write to Dr. McKeever in the space below.

Also, on the reverse side are shown some of his other materials and services.

Comments:

TO:
DR. JAMES McKEEVER
OMEGA MINISTRIES
P. O. BOX 4130
MEDFORD, OR 97501 USA

Dear Dr. McKeever,
I am enclosing:

☐ $________ for additional copies of JESUS—FOR THE *REST* OF YOUR LIFE (for a contribution of $1.95 each)

☐ $________ for your ministry in general

☐ $________ Total contribution enclosed
(make check payable to Omega Ministries)

☐ I will be praying for your ministry

NAME ____

ADDRESS _____________________________________

CITY ____

STATE __________________ ZIP ____________

PHONE _______________________________________

Also send me information on the following materials by Dr. James McKeever:

☐ Other booklets in this series
☐ The Christian newsletter that he edits, *End-Times News Digest (END)*
☐ Books by him
☐ Cassettes of his speaking ministry
☐ Information about his speaking at our church or Christian conference
☐ Please read comments on other side